con

M000012985

British & North American Readers:
Please note that Australian cup and
spoon measurements are metric. A quick
conversion guide appears on page 63.
A glossary explaining unfamiliar terms
and ingredients begins on page 60.

2 What you need to know...

Before you begin, quickly read this important information to guarantee your cake or pudding realises its full and delicious potential.

Lining cake pans

To line the sides of a cake pan, cut three strips of baking paper long enough to fit around the pan and 8cm wider than the depth of the pan. Fold strips lengthways about 2cm from edge and make diagonal cuts about 2cm apart up to the fold. Fit around the curves or corners of the pan, with cut section resting on the base. Using base of pan as a guide, cut three paper shapes to cover base of pan; place paper bases in position.

Filling cake pan

Spoon small amounts of cake mixture into corners of prepared pan, holding paper in position. Spread remaining mixture firmly into pan; smooth top with spatula or damp hand. Hold pan about 15cm above the kitchen bench; drop pan firmly onto bench to release air bubbles and settle mixture.

To test if cake is cooked

After minimum cooking time, feel top of cake with fingertips. If cake feels firm, gently push a sharp vegetable knife into the thickest part of the cake, as close to the centre as possible, right through to the base of pan. Gently withdraw knife and feel the blade; if the blade is simply sticky from fruit, the cake is cooked, but if there is moist cake mixture on the blade, return the cake to oven for a further 15 minutes before testing again.

When cake is cooked

Make cuts in lining paper level with pan, fold down paper. Cover hot cake with foil, wrap in towel; cool in pan.

Lining cake pan

Smoothing mixture with spatula

Testing if cake is cooked

To store cake

When cake has completely cooled, remove from pan. Leaving lining paper intact, wrap in plastic wrap. Place cake in airtight container or plastic freezer bag. Store in a cool place or freeze.

Cake hints

The cake mixture can be made ahead – place cake mixture into prepared pan, cover the surface with plastic wrap and refrigerate for 2 days. Stand mixture about 3 hours to return to room temperature before baking. Cold mixture will take about 30 minutes longer to cook.

To store puddings

If pudding is calico-wrapped, hang pudding for 10 minutes after initial cooking. Remove cloth and allow to cool. Then, for all pudding recipes, wrap cooled pudding in plastic wrap and seal in freezer bag or an airtight container; refrigerate or freeze.

Reheating puddings

Three days before you want to use a frozen pudding, place it in the refrigerator to thaw. Remove pudding from refrigerator 12 hours before reheating.

Traditional steamed pudding: Remove plastic wrap, return pudding to steamer and prepare as for cooking method. Steam for 2 hours.

Traditional boiled pudding: Remove plastic wrap and tie a clean, dry, unfloured cloth on pudding. Boil 2 hours as for cooking method. Hang hot pudding 10 minutes, remove cloth. Stand pudding 20 minutes for skin to darken.

Pudding in the microwave: Reheat four single serves at once. Cover with plastic wrap, microwave on HIGH (100%) for up to 1 minute per serve. To reheat whole, cover with plastic wrap, microwave on MEDIUM (50%) about 15 minutes or until hot.

4 golden glacé fruit cake

250g butter

1 cup (220g) caster sugar

4 eggs

1 cup (190g) mixed dried fruit

¾ cup (185g) quartered glacé cherries

½ cup (125g) chopped glacé apricots

⅓ cup (85g) chopped glacé peaches

½ cup (115g) chopped glacé pineapple

¾ cup (125g) blanched almonds, toasted, halved

1 cup (150g) plain flour

1 cup (150g) self-raising flour

¼ cup (60ml) Cointreau

¼ cup (60ml) apricot jam

extra blanched almonds, to decorate

Grease deep 23cm-round cake pan or deep 19cm-square cake pan, line base and side(s) with three layers baking paper, extending paper 5cm above edge of pan.

Beat butter and sugar in large bowl with electric mixer until changed to a lighter colour. Add eggs, one at a time, beating until just combined between additions (mixture may curdle). Stir in fruit, nuts, flours, Cointreau and jam.

Spread cake mixture into prepared pan; decorate top with extra blanched almonds, if desired. Bake in moderately slow oven about 2 hours. Cover hot cake tightly with foil; cool in pan.

SERVES 36
Per serving 9.1g fat; 845kJ

6 healthy low-fat fruit cake

You will need to cook about 400g peeled pumpkin for this recipe.

2³/₄ cups (500g) mixed dried fruit

1 cup (250ml) apricot nectar

1 teaspoon honey

1 cup (250g) mashed pumpkin

1¹/₂ cups (225g) self-raising flour

1 teaspoon mixed spice

1 teaspoon bicarbonate of soda

Combine fruit, nectar and honey in medium saucepan, bring to a boil; simmer, uncovered, 3 minutes. Transfer mixture to large heatproof bowl; cool.

Grease 14cm x 21cm loaf pan, cover base with baking paper.

Stir pumpkin and sifted dry ingredients into fruit mixture. Spread cake mixture into prepared pan; bake in moderate oven about 1 hour. Cover hot cake tightly with foil; cool in pan.

SERVES 24
Per serving 0.3g fat; 402kJ

chocolate chip fruit cake

2¹/₃ cups (375g)
sultanas

1 cup (210g) glacé
cherries, halved

1 cup (250g) chopped
glacé apricots

150g dark chocolate,
chopped coarsely

185g butter,
chopped coarsely

³/₄ cup (150g) firmly
packed brown sugar

1 cup (250ml)
sweet sherry

4 eggs, beaten lightly

150g dark Choc Bits

1³/₄ cups (260g)
plain flour

¹/₄ cup (35g)
self-raising flour

¹/₂ teaspoon
bicarbonate of soda

2 tablespoons sweet
sherry, extra

Combine fruit, chopped chocolate, butter,
sugar and sherry in large saucepan. Stir over
heat, without boiling, until chocolate and
butter melt. Simmer, uncovered, 10 minutes.
Transfer mixture to large heatproof bowl,
cool to room temperature.

Grease deep 19cm-square cake pan, line
base and sides with three layers baking paper,
extending paper 5cm above edge of pan.

Stir egg, Choc Bits and sifted dry ingredients
into fruit mixture. Spread cake mixture into
prepared pan; bake in slow oven about
2 hours. Brush top of hot cake with extra
sherry, cover tightly with foil; cool in pan.

SERVES 30
Per serving 8.9g fat; 1044kJ

8 ginger and orange
liqueur cake

½ cup (115g) glacé ginger, chopped finely

1½ cups (250g) sultanas

1½ cups (250g) chopped seeded dates

1 cup (170g) mixed peel

½ cup (125ml) Grand Marnier

250g butter

1 teaspoon finely grated orange rind

1 cup (200g) firmly packed brown sugar

4 eggs

1½ cups (225g) plain flour

1 teaspoon ground ginger

Combine glacé ginger, fruit and Grand Marnier in large bowl, cover; stand overnight.

Grease deep 20cm-round cake pan, line base and side with three layers baking paper, extending paper 5cm above edge of pan.

Beat butter, rind and sugar in medium bowl with electric mixer until combined. Add eggs, one at a time, beating until just combined between additions. Stir butter mixture into fruit mixture, then stir in flour and ground ginger.

Spread cake mixture into prepared pan; bake in slow oven about 2½ hours. Cover hot cake tightly with foil; cool in pan. Decorate cake with Marzipan Oranges, if desired.

Marzipan Oranges Buy a 200g roll of marzipan from health food store (some supermarkets also stock it). Dust hands well with sifted pure icing sugar. Roll pieces of marzipan into balls for oranges, place small part of clove in position on oranges. Gently roll oranges over grater to give effect of orange skin. Stand oranges on wire rack to dry overnight. Paint with orange food colouring; leave to dry overnight.

SERVES 25
Per serving 9.3g fat; 1064kJ

10 condensed milk

fruit cake

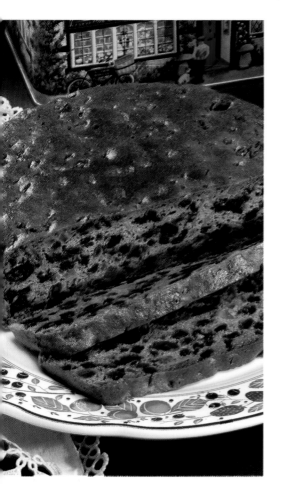

4 cups (750g) mixed
dried fruit

1/2 cup (125ml) water

1 cup (150g)
self-raising flour

1 egg

400g can (300ml) sweetened
condensed milk

Cook fruit and the water in
large saucepan, stirring,
until mixture comes to a boil.
Simmer, uncovered, 1 minute.
Transfer mixture to large
heatproof bowl, cover;
cool to room temperature.
Grease deep 20cm-round
cake pan, line base and
side with three layers baking
paper, extending paper
5cm above edge of pan.
Stir remaining ingredients
into fruit mixture. Spread
cake mixture into prepared
pan; bake in slow oven
about 2 hours. Cover
hot cake tightly with foil;
cool in pan.

SERVES 25
Per serving 2g fat; 645kJ

fruit cake

2¹/₃ cups (375g) sultanas

2¹/₄ cups (375g) chopped raisins

³/₄ cup (110g) dried currants

¹/₂ cup (105g) glacé cherries, halved

250g butter, chopped coarsely

1 cup (200g) firmly packed brown sugar

¹/₂ cup (125ml) sweet sherry

¹/₄ cup (60ml) water

1 tablespoon treacle

2 teaspoons finely grated orange rind

2 teaspoons finely lemon rind

5 eggs, beaten lightly

1³/₄ cups (260g) plain flour

¹/₃ cup (50g) self-raising flour

extra glacé cherries, to decorate

Combine fruit, butter, sugar, sherry and the water in large saucepan. Stir over heat, without boiling, until butter melts and sugar dissolves. Bring to a boil, then remove from heat. Transfer mixture to large heatproof bowl; cool.

Grease deep 19cm-square cake pan or deep 23cm-round cake pan, line base and sides with three layers baking paper, extending paper 5cm above edge of pan.

Stir treacle, rinds and egg into fruit mixture, then stir in flours. Spread cake mixture into prepared pan; decorate top with extra glacé cherries, if desired. Bake in slow oven about 2³/₄ hours. Cover hot cake tightly with foil; cool in pan.

SERVES 36
Per serving 6.7g fat; 850kJ

12 marsala

pistachio cake

1³/₄ cups (375g) red glacé cherries, quartered

1 cup (160g) sultanas

³/₄ cup (125g) chopped raisins

1 cup (170g) mixed peel

1¹/₂ teaspoons fennel seeds, crushed

1 tablespoon finely grated orange rind

2 teaspoons finely grated lemon rind

¹/₂ cup (125ml) marsala

250g butter

³/₄ cup (165g) caster sugar

5 eggs

¹/₃ cup (50g) shelled pistachios

1¹/₂ cups (225g) plain flour

¹/₄ cup (35g) self-raising flour

to decorate

200g roll marzipan

green food colouring

1 tablespoon apricot jam

2 teaspoons sweet sherry

pure icing sugar

500g packet soft icing

red food colouring

Combine fruit, seeds, rinds and marsala in large bowl, cover; stand overnight.
Grease deep 20cm-round cake pan, line base and side with three layers baking paper, extending paper 5cm above edge of pan.
Beat butter and sugar in medium bowl with electric mixer until changed to a lighter colour. Add eggs, one at a time, beating until just combined between additions (mixture may curdle). Stir into fruit mixture, mix well, then stir in nuts and flours, in two batches.
Spread cake mixture into prepared pan; bake in moderately slow oven about 2 hours. Cover hot cake tightly with foil; cool in pan.
To Decorate Colour three-quarters of the marzipan with green food colouring. Brush top of cake with a little of combined sieved warm jam and sherry. Roll out green marzipan on surface which has been dusted lightly with sifted icing sugar until large enough to cover top of cake, place on cake; trim edge. Roll out soft icing until large enough to cover marzipan, place on top of marzipan; trim edge. Cut leaves from remaining green marzipan. Brush edge of cake with sherry mixture, decorate with leaves. Colour remaining marzipan with red food colouring, shape into balls, decorate as shown.

SERVES 25
Per serving 7.8g fat; 1352kJ

14 coconut fruit cake

185g butter, chopped coarsely

2 teaspoons coconut essence

1/2 cup (110g) caster sugar

3 eggs

1 cup (90g) desiccated coconut

1/2 cup (75g) plain flour

1/2 cup (75g) self-raising flour

1/2 cup (125ml) coconut milk

1 cup (190g) chopped dried figs

3/4 cup (185g) chopped glacé apricots

2/3 cup (110g) sultanas

2/3 cup (110g) mixed peel

Grease deep 20cm-round cake pan, line base and side with three layers baking paper, extending paper 5cm above edge of pan.
Combine butter, essence, sugar, eggs, coconut, flours and coconut milk in medium bowl of electric mixer, beat on low speed until ingredients are combined. Then, beat on medium speed until mixture has changed to a lighter colour. Stir in fruit.
Spread cake mixture into prepared pan; bake in slow oven about 2 hours. Cover hot cake tightly with foil; cool in pan.

SERVES 25
Per serving 10.2g fat; 795kJ

2¹/₃ cups (375g) sultanas

1¹/₂ cups (250g) raisins, chopped coarsely

1²/₃ cups (250g) dried currants

³/₄ cup (125g) mixed peel

¹/₂ cup (105g) glacé cherries, halved

¹/₄ cup (55g) chopped glacé pineapple

¹/₄ cup (60g) chopped glacé apricots

250g butter, chopped coarsely

1 cup (200g) firmly packed brown sugar

¹/₂ cup (125ml) brandy

¹/₂ cup (125ml) water

2 teaspoons finely grated orange rind

1 teaspoon finely grated lemon rind

1 tablespoon treacle

5 eggs, beaten lightly

1³/₄ cups (260g) plain flour

¹/₃ cup (50g) self-raising flour

¹/₂ teaspoon bicarbonate of soda

Combine fruit, butter, sugar, brandy and the water in large saucepan. Stir over heat, without boiling, until butter melts and sugar dissolves. Bring to a boil, then remove from heat. Transfer mixture to large heatproof bowl; cool.
Grease deep 23cm-round cake pan, line base and side with three layers baking paper, extending paper 5cm above edge of pan.
Stir rinds, treacle and egg into fruit mixture, then stir in sifted dry ingredients, in two batches. Spread cake mixture into prepared pan; bake in slow oven about 2¹/₂ hours. Cover hot cake tightly with foil; cool in pan.

SERVES 36
Per serving 6.7g fat; 900kJ

16 grand marnier
fruit cake

This is one of our more extravagant recipes. The dried fruit is soaked for 10 days in the orange-flavoured liqueur, giving the cake its deliciously special taste.

3 cups (500g) sultanas

1½ cups (250g) mixed peel

¾ cup (125g) chopped raisins

¾ cup (125g) chopped seeded dates

⅔ cup (140g) chopped seeded prunes

½ cup (125g) chopped glacé apricots

⅔ cup (150g) chopped glacé pineapple

½ cup (70g) slivered almonds

½ cup (60g) chopped walnuts

1 tablespoon finely grated orange rind

½ cup (110g) caster sugar

¼ cup (60ml) orange juice

½ cup (125ml) Grand Marnier

250g butter, softened

½ cup (100g) firmly packed brown sugar

5 eggs

2 cups (300g) plain flour

2 tablespoons Grand Marnier, extra

Combine fruit in jar or large container with tight-fitting lid; mix in nuts and rind.
Sprinkle caster sugar evenly into large heavy-base frying pan. Cook, over low heat, without stirring, until sugar begins to melt; at that point, immediately begin stirring until sugar is completely melted and golden brown. Remove from heat, stir in juice. Return to heat, stirring constantly, until toffee-like pieces have dissolved. Do not boil or mixture will evaporate. Stir in liqueur, then strain into jug; discard any small pieces of toffee. Pour over fruit mixture in jar; cover tightly with lid.
Next day, turn jar upside down; do this daily for 10 days.
The day of baking, grease deep 23cm-round cake pan, line base and side with three layers baking paper, extending paper 5cm above edge of pan.
Beat butter and brown sugar in medium bowl with electric mixer until combined; add eggs, one at a time, beating until just combined between additions. Combine fruit mixture and butter mixture in large bowl; add flour, mix well.
Spread cake mixture into prepared pan; bake in slow oven about 3½ hours. Brush top of hot cake with extra Grand Marnier, cover tightly with foil; cool in pan.

SERVES 36
Per serving 8.9g fat; 1072kJ

18 rum and citrus
fruit cake

1½ cups (315g) red glacé cherries, quartered

½ cup (125g) chopped glacé apricots

¾ cup (125g) sultanas

¾ cup (110g) dried currants

½ cup (80g) chopped blanched almonds

1 tablespoon finely grated orange rind

2 teaspoons finely grated lemon rind

2 tablespoons rum

250g butter

¾ cup (165g) caster sugar

5 eggs

1½ cups (225g) plain flour

¼ cup (35g) self-raising flour

Combine fruit, nuts, rinds and rum in large bowl, cover; stand overnight.

Grease deep 20cm-round cake pan, line base and side with three layers baking paper, extending paper 5cm above edge of pan.

Beat butter and sugar in medium bowl with electric mixer until changed to a lighter colour. Add eggs, one at a time, beating until just combined between additions (mixture may curdle). Stir into fruit mixture, mix well; stir in flours, in two batches.

Spread cake mixture into prepared pan; bake in moderately slow oven about 2 hours. Cover hot cake tightly with foil; cool in pan.

SERVES 25
Per serving 11.2g fat; 575kJ

cream cheese

fruit cake

90g butter,
chopped coarsely

125g packet
cream cheese,
chopped coarsely

³/₄ cup (165g)
caster sugar

2 eggs

¹/₂ cup (75g) plain flour

¹/₂ cup (75g) self-
raising flour

¹/₄ cup (60ml) brandy

1¹/₂ cups (315g)
chopped seeded
prunes

³/₄ cup (185g) chopped
glacé apricots

Grease deep 20cm-round cake pan, line base and side
with three layers baking paper, extending paper 5cm above
edge of pan.
Combine butter, cheese, sugar, eggs, flours and brandy
in medium bowl of electric mixer, beat on low speed until
ingredients are combined. Then, beat on medium speed until
mixture is smooth and changed to a lighter colour. Stir in fruit.
Spread cake mixture into prepared pan; bake in slow oven
about 2¹/₂ hours. Cover hot cake tightly with foil; cool in pan.

SERVES 25
Per serving 5.1g fat; 594kJ

20 date and nut cakes

This recipe contains no flour. Cake will slice easily if refrigerated for several hours.

²/₃ cup (110g) seeded dates, halved

¹/₂ cup (95g) dried figs, quartered

¹/₃ cup (55g) mixed peel

¹/₂ cup (105g) red glacé cherries, halved

¹/₂ cup (105g) green glacé cherries, halved

¹/₂ cup (85g) raisins

¹/₃ cup (75g) glacé ginger, chopped coarsely

1¹/₂ cups (240g) blanched almonds

1¹/₂ cups (150g) pecans

1¹/₄ cups (155g) almond meal

¹/₂ teaspoon baking powder

4 eggs

¹/₄ cup (60ml) honey

2 tablespoons dark rum

Grease two 8cm x 26cm bar cake pans; line bases and sides with three layers baking paper, extending paper 5cm above edge of pans.
Place fruit, ginger and whole nuts in large bowl; stir in almond meal and baking powder. Beat eggs in small bowl with electric mixer until thick and creamy; beat in honey. Stir egg mixture into fruit mixture.
Spread cake mixture into prepared pans. Using slightly wet hands, press mixture firmly into pans. Bake in slow oven about 1¹/₄ hours. Brush tops of hot cakes with rum, cover tightly with foil; cool in pans.

MAKES 2 cakes (serves 30)
Per serving 5.8g fat; 391kJ

non-dairy **fruit** cake 21

2³/₄ cups (500g)
mixed dried fruit

1 cup (150g) finely
chopped dried apricots

440g can crushed
pineapple in
natural juice

¹/₄ cup (60ml) freshly
squeezed orange juice

1 teaspoon
mixed spice

¹/₄ teaspoon
ground cloves

1 teaspoon
bicarbonate of soda

2 egg whites

2 cups (320g)
wholemeal
self-raising flour

Cook dried fruits, undrained pineapple, juice
and spices in large saucepan, stirring, until
mixture comes to a boil. Simmer, stirring,
5 minutes. Transfer to large heatproof bowl,
cover; cool.
Grease deep 20cm-round cake pan, line
base and side with three layers baking paper,
extending paper 5cm above edge of pan.
Stir sifted soda and egg whites into fruit
mixture, then fold in flour (mixture will be firm).
Spread cake mixture into prepared pan; using
wet hands, pat down top of cake. Bake
in moderately slow oven about 1¹/₂ hours.
Cover hot cake tightly with foil; cool in pan.

SERVES 30
Per serving 0.4g fat; 406kJ

22 traditional fruit cake

2 cups (300g) currants

2 cups (340g) raisins, chopped coarsely

3 cups (500g) sultanas

1/2 cup (125ml) dark rum

150g butter

1 cup (200g) firmly packed brown sugar

4 eggs

1/2 cup (125ml) strawberry jam

1 cup (210g) glacé cherries, chopped coarsely

2 cups (340g) mixed peel

1 cup (140g) slivered almonds

2 cups (300g) plain flour

1/2 cup (75g) self-raising flour

1/2 teaspoon ground cinnamon

1/2 teaspoon ground allspice

blanched almonds and extra glacé cherries, to decorate

1/4 cup (60ml) dark rum, extra

Combine dried fruit and rum in large bowl, cover; stand overnight.

Grease deep 23cm-round cake pan, line base and side with three layers baking paper, extending paper 5cm above edge of pan.

Beat butter and sugar in small bowl with electric mixer until combined. Add eggs, one at a time, beating until just combined between additions; stir in jam. Stir into fruit mixture, then stir in cherries, peel, slivered almonds and sifted dry ingredients.

Spread cake mixture into prepared pan; decorate top with blanched almonds and extra glacé cherries, if desired. Bake in slow oven about 3 hours. Brush top of hot cake with extra rum, cover tightly with foil; cool in pan.

SERVES 36
Per serving 7.2g fat; 1184kJ

24 wholemeal honey beer fruit cake

250g butter,
chopped coarsely

1¼ cups (310ml)
honey

3 eggs

1½ cups (240g)
wholemeal
self-raising flour

1½ cups (240g)
wholemeal plain flour

1 teaspoon
mixed spice

1½ cups (250g)
chopped raisins

1½ cups (250g)
chopped seeded dates

1½ cups (250g)
sultanas

¾ cup (125g)
mixed peel

¾ cup (110g) chopped
dried apricots

⅓ cup (65g) chopped
glacé ginger

¼ cup (50g) glacé
cherries, quartered

375ml can beer

Grease deep 23cm-square cake pan, line
base and sides with three layers baking paper,
extending paper 5cm above edge of pan.
Combine butter, honey, eggs, flours and spice
in large bowl of electric mixer, beat on low
speed until ingredients are combined. Then,
beat on medium speed until mixture is smooth
and changed to a lighter colour. Stir in
remaining ingredients.
Spread cake mixture into prepared pan; bake
in slow oven about 2¾ hours. Cover hot cake
tightly with foil; cool in pan.

SERVES 48
Per serving 4.9g fat; 709kJ

honeyed glacé
fruit cake

250g butter,
chopped coarsely

2 tablespoons honey

1 cup (220g)
caster sugar

4 eggs

1/4 cup (60ml)
sweet sherry

1 1/2 cups (225g)
plain flour

3/4 cup (110g)
self-raising flour

1/2 cup (115g) finely
chopped glacé
pineapple

1/2 cup (105g)
glacé cherries,
chopped coarsely

1/4 cup (60g)
finely chopped
glacé apricots

1 cup (200g) finely
chopped glacé ginger

Grease deep 19cm-square cake pan, line
base and sides with three layers baking paper,
extending paper 5cm above edge of pan.
Combine butter, honey, sugar, eggs, sherry and
flours in large bowl of electric mixer, beat on
low speed until ingredients are combined. Then,
beat on medium speed until mixture is smooth
and slightly lighter in colour (do not over-beat).
Stir in fruit and ginger.
Spread cake mixture into prepared pan; bake
in slow oven about 2 1/2 hours. Cover hot cake
tightly with foil; cool in pan.

SERVES 30
Per serving 7.7g fat; 794kJ

26 bourbon and maple
fruit cake

3 cups (500g) sultanas

2¹/₄ cups (375g)
chopped raisins

1¹/₂ cups (250g) chopped
seeded dates

³/₄ cup (155g) chopped
seeded prunes

¹/₂ cup (125ml)
maple syrup

²/₃ cup (160ml) bourbon

250g butter

1¹/₃ cups (275g) firmly
packed brown sugar

4 eggs

2 cups (300g) plain flour

1 teaspoon
ground nutmeg

1 teaspoon
ground cinnamon

1 cup (125g) chopped
toasted pecans

extra pecans, to decorate

maple glaze

3 teaspoons gelatine

1 tablespoon
boiling water

¹/₄ cup (60ml)
maple syrup

Combine fruit, maple syrup and bourbon in large bowl, cover; stand overnight or up to a week.

Grease deep 23cm-round cake pan or deep 19cm-square cake pan, line base and side with three layers baking paper, extending paper 5cm above edge of pan.

Beat butter and sugar in medium bowl with electric mixer until changed to a lighter colour. Add eggs, one at a time, beating until just combined between additions (mixture may curdle). Stir into fruit mixture; mix well, then stir in flour, spices and chopped pecans.

Spread cake mixture into prepared pan; decorate top with extra pecans, if desired. Bake in slow oven about 3 hours. Cover hot cake tightly with foil; cool in pan. Brush cake with Maple Glaze the day before serving.

Maple Glaze Combine gelatine and boiling water in small bowl; stir until gelatine is dissolved. Stir in syrup.

SERVES 36
Per serving 10g fat; 1163kJ

28 brandied light

fruit cake

1¹/₄ cups (185g)
plain flour

1¹/₄ cups (185g)
self-raising flour

185g butter,
chopped coarsely

4 cups (750g) mixed
dried fruit

³/₄ cup (165g)
raw sugar

³/₄ cup (180ml)
hot milk

2 tablespoons brandy

2 eggs, beaten lightly

Grease deep 20cm-round cake pan,
line base and side with three layers baking
paper, extending paper 5cm above edge
of pan.
Combine flours in large bowl; rub in butter,
then stir in remaining ingredients.
Spread cake mixture into prepared pan;
bake in slow oven about 2¹/₂ hours. Cover
hot cake tightly with foil; cool in pan.

SERVES 30
Per serving 6g fat; 782kJ

spiced potato
fruit cake

You will need to cook
1 large (300g) potato
for this recipe.

185g butter,
chopped coarsely

2 tablespoons
golden syrup

1 cup (220g)
raw sugar

2¾ cups (500g)
mixed dried fruit

1 cup cold cooked
mashed potato

2 eggs

1 cup (150g)
self-raising flour

1 cup (150g)
plain flour

1 teaspoon
mixed spice

1 teaspoon
ground nutmeg

Combine butter, golden syrup, sugar and fruit
in medium saucepan. Stir over heat, without
boiling, until butter melts. Transfer mixture to
large heatproof bowl, cool slightly. Stir in potato
and eggs, cover; cool.
Grease deep 20cm-round cake pan, line
base and side with three layers baking paper,
extending paper 5cm above edge of pan.
Stir sifted flours and spices into fruit mixture.
Spread cake mixture into prepared pan; bake
in moderately slow oven about 2 hours. Cover
hot cake tightly with foil; cool in pan.

SERVES 25
Per serving 7.4g fat; 854kJ

30 spicy ginger boiled fruit cake

1³/₄ cups (280g) sultanas

³/₄ cup (125g) chopped raisins

³/₄ cup (125g) chopped
seeded dates

¹/₂ cup (85g) mixed peel,
chopped finely

¹/₂ cup (115g) glacé ginger,
chopped finely

185g butter, chopped

¹/₂ cup (100g) firmly packed
brown sugar

¹/₃ cup (80ml) golden syrup

¹/₂ cup (125ml) sweet sherry

2 eggs, beaten lightly

1 cup (150g) plain flour

1 cup (150g) self-raising flour

2 teaspoons ground ginger

1 teaspoon mixed spice

¹/₂ teaspoon bicarbonate of soda

1 cup (125g) chopped pecans

glacé fruit and extra pecans,
to decorate

2 tablespoons sweet sherry, extra

glaze

2 teaspoons gelatine

2 tablespoons water

1 tablespoon sugar

Combine fruit, ginger, butter, sugar, golden syrup and sherry in large saucepan. Stir over heat, without boiling, until butter melts and sugar dissolves. Simmer, uncovered, 3 minutes. Transfer mixture to large heatproof bowl; cool to room temperature.

Grease deep 19cm-square cake pan, line base and sides with three layers baking paper, extending paper 5cm above edge of pan.

Stir egg, sifted dry ingredients and chopped pecans into fruit mixture, in two batches. Spread cake mixture into prepared pan; decorate top with glacé fruit and extra pecans, if desired. Bake in slow oven about 2¹/₄ hours. Brush top of hot cake with extra sherry, cover tightly with foil; cool in pan. Brush cold cake with Glaze, stand until set.

Glaze Sprinkle gelatine over the water in cup, add sugar; stand in small pan of simmering water, stir until dissolved.

SERVES 36
Per serving 8.2g fat; 829kJ

Four quick **toppings**

for puddings

These Christmas pudding accompaniments are so delectable you might have to make all four! The recipes for hard sauce will freeze successfully for up to 4 weeks, covered tightly. The other recipes are best made just before serving.

cinnamon rum hard sauce

250g soft butter

1 cup (200g) firmly packed brown sugar

2 teaspoons ground cinnamon

2 tablespoons dark rum

Beat butter, sugar and cinnamon in small bowl with electric mixer until light and fluffy; add rum, beat until combined. Spoon mixture into piping bag fitted with medium fluted tube. Pipe mixture into twelve 5cm rounds on plastic-wrap-lined tray. Refrigerate until firm.

SERVES 12
Per serving 17.2g fat; 926kJ

easy coffee sauce

1 litre vanilla ice-cream

2 tablespoons dry instant coffee

1 tablespoon boiling water

Stand ice-cream at room temperature until melted. Dissolve coffee and boiling water in small bowl; stir into melted ice-cream.

SERVES 8
Per serving 6.9g fat; 494kJ

orange liqueur hard sauce

125g soft butter

2 teaspoons finely grated orange rind

½ cup (80g) pure icing sugar

2 tablespoons Irish cream liqueur

Beat butter and rind in small bowl with electric mixer until light and fluffy; gradually add sifted icing sugar, beat until smooth. Add liqueur, beat until combined. Spoon mixture into serving bowl.

SERVES 6
Per serving 1.8g fat; 946kJ

caramel rum custard

600ml carton prepared vanilla custard

1 tablespoon dark rum

¾ cup (150g) firmly packed brown sugar

2 teaspoons vanilla essence

Combine custard, rum and sugar in medium saucepan; stir over low heat until sugar is dissolved. Stir in essence. Serve warm or cold.

SERVES 6
Per serving 3.6g fat; 906kJ

brandied
sultana cake

4¹/₂ cups (750g) sultanas

250g butter

1 cup (220g) caster sugar

5 eggs

2¹/₂ cups (375g) plain flour

¹/₄ cup (35g) self-raising flour

¹/₄ cup (60ml) brandy

Place sultanas in large bowl, cover with warm water; stand 2 hours, drain. Place sultanas on absorbent paper on tray, cover with absorbent paper; stand overnight.

Grease deep 23cm-round cake pan, line base and side with three layers baking paper, extending paper 5cm above edge of pan.

Beat butter and sugar in large bowl with electric mixer until changed to a lighter colour. Add eggs, one at a time, beating until just combined between additions (mixture may curdle). Stir in flours, brandy and sultanas, in two batches.

Spread cake mixture into prepared pan; bake in moderately slow oven about 2 hours. Cover hot cake tightly with foil; cool in pan.

SERVES 36
Per serving 6.6g fat; 799kJ

multipurpose
fruit cake

1¹/₂ cups (250g) sultanas

1¹/₂ cups (250g) chopped raisins

²/₃ cup (140g) chopped seeded prunes

³/₄ cup (110g) dried currants

¹/₂ cup (125g) chopped glacé apricots

²/₃ cup (110g) chopped seeded dates

¹/₄ cup (60g) chopped glacé cherries

¹/₂ cup (125ml) brandy

250g butter

2 teaspoons finely grated lemon rind

1 cup (200g) firmly packed brown sugar

2 tablespoons honey

4 eggs

1¹/₂ cups (225g) plain flour

¹/₂ cup (75g) self-raising flour

1 teaspoon mixed spice

¹/₄ cup (60ml) brandy, extra

Combine fruit and brandy in large bowl, cover; stand overnight or up to a week.

Grease a deep 23cm-round cake pan or a deep 19cm-square cake pan; line base and side(s) with three layers baking paper, extending paper 5cm above edge of pan.

Beat butter, rind and sugar in medium bowl with electric mixer until combined; add honey, beat until just combined. Add eggs, one at a time, beating until just combined between additions. Stir into fruit mixture, then stir in sifted flours and spice.

Spread cake mixture into prepared pan. Bake in slow oven 3 hours. Brush hot cake with extra brandy, cover tightly with foil; cool in pan.

SERVES 36
Per serving 6.5g fat; 843kJ
Tip Substitute 1kg mixed dried fruit for the fruit listed.

weekly fruit cake

The most popular of all our fruit cakes, this traditional stand-by keeps and cuts well – so it can double as a spectacular wedding cake too. Sherry or brandy can be substituted for rum, if preferred.

3 cups (500g) sultanas

1½ cups (250g) raisins, chopped coarsely

⅔ cup (140g) red glacé cherries, quartered

¾ cup (110g) dried currants

¾ cup (125g) mixed peel

2 tablespoons marmalade

½ cup (125ml) rum

250g butter, softened

1 teaspoon finely grated orange rind

1 teaspoon finely grated lemon rind

1 cup (200g) firmly packed brown sugar

4 eggs

2 cups (300g) plain flour

2 teaspoons mixed spice

blanched almonds, to decorate

2 tablespoons rum, extra

Grease deep 23cm-round cake pan, line base and side with three layers baking paper, extending paper 5cm above edge of pan.
Combine fruit, marmalade and rum in large bowl. Beat butter, rinds and sugar in medium bowl with electric mixer until just combined. Add eggs, one at a time, beating until just combined between additions. Stir butter mixture into fruit mixture; mix in flour and spice.
Spread cake mixture into prepared pan; decorate top with blanched almonds. Bake in slow oven about 3½ hours. Brush top of hot cake with extra rum, cover tightly with foil; cool in pan.

SERVES 36
Per serving 7.3g fat; 919kJ

38 country fruit cake

1 1/2 cups (225g)
dried currants

1 cup (160g) sultanas

1 cup (170g)
chopped raisins

1/3 cup (75g) chopped
glacé pineapple

1/3 cup (85g) chopped
glacé apricots

1/3 cup (55g)
mixed peel

1/3 cup (85g) chopped
glacé cherries

3/4 cup (125g)
chopped Brazil nuts

3/4 cup (180ml) brandy

185g butter, softened

1 cup (200g) firmly
packed brown sugar

3 eggs

2 tablespoons
strawberry jam

2 cups (300g)
plain flour

1 teaspoon ground
cinnamon

1 teaspoon
ground nutmeg

1 teaspoon
ground ginger

1/4 cup (60ml)
brandy, extra

Combine fruit, nuts and brandy in large bowl; cover, stand overnight.

Grease deep 19cm-square cake pan, line base and sides with three layers of baking paper, extending paper 5cm above edge of pan.

Beat butter and sugar in small bowl with electric mixer until just combined. Add eggs, one at a time, beating until just combined between additions; stir in jam. Stir into fruit mixture, then stir in sifted dry ingredients.

Spread cake mixture into prepared pan; bake in slow oven about 3 1/2 hours. Brush top of hot cake with extra brandy, cover tightly with foil; cool in pan.

SERVES 36
Per serving 7.3g fat; 837kJ

fruit cake

2³/₄ cups (500g) mixed
dried fruit

1 cup (250ml) water

¹/₂ cup (100g) firmly
packed brown sugar

60g butter

¹/₃ cup (55g) chopped
seeded dates

1 cup (150g)
plain flour

¹/₂ cup (75g)
self-raising flour

1 teaspoon
bicarbonate of soda

1 teaspoon
mixed spice

¹/₄ cup (60ml)
sweet sherry

Combine dried fruit, the water, sugar and butter in medium saucepan.
Stir over heat, without boiling, until sugar dissolves. Simmer, uncovered,
3 minutes. Transfer mixture to large heatproof bowl, stir in dates; cool.
Grease deep 19cm-square cake pan, line base and sides with three
layers baking paper, extending paper 5cm above edge of pan.
Stir sifted dry ingredients and sherry into fruit mixture, in two batches.
Spread cake mixture into prepared pan; bake in slow oven about
2¹/₄ hours. Cover hot cake tightly with foil; cool in pan.

SERVES 36
Per serving 1.6g fat; 368kJ

40 suet

christmas pudding

You will need to buy 200g fresh suet from the butcher; it may be necessary to order it in advance. Remove all sinew and membrane from suet before grating. Suet can be chopped finely by processing with the flour instead of grating. See page 3 for details on how to store and reheat puddings.

1¹/₂ cups (250g) raisins, chopped coarsely

1¹/₂ cups (250g) sultanas

³/₄ cup (110g) dried currants

³/₄ cup (125g) mixed peel

¹/₃ cup (55g) blanched almonds, chopped finely

¹/₃ cup (80ml) brandy

¹/₃ cup (80ml) beer

2 teaspoons finely grated orange rind

¹/₄ cup (60ml) orange juice

175g fresh suet, grated coarsely

¹/₂ cup (100g) firmly packed brown sugar

1 cup (150g) self-raising flour

2¹/₂ cups (175g) stale breadcrumbs

1 small (130g) apple, peeled, grated coarsely

¹/₂ teaspoon ground cinnamon

¹/₂ teaspoon ground nutmeg

¹/₂ teaspoon ground allspice

3 eggs, beaten lightly

Combine fruit, nuts, brandy, beer, rind and juice in large bowl, cover; stand overnight at room temperature.
Stir in suet, sugar, flour, breadcrumbs, apple and spices until well combined. Stir in egg.
Place mixture into prepared floured cloth or greased 2.25-litre (9-cup) pudding basin.
Boil or steam pudding 4 hours.

SERVES 12
Per serving 17.6g fat; 2039kJ

42 fruit mince layer cake

Cake can be made up to 3 days ahead, or frozen for up to 2 months. Defrost on day of serving.

125g butter, softened

1 teaspoon vanilla essence

3/4 cup (165g) caster sugar

2 eggs

1 1/2 cups (225g) self-raising flour

1/2 cup (125ml) milk

filling

30g butter

1/4 cup (55g) caster sugar

1 tablespoon brandy

1 tablespoon water

1 egg, beaten lightly

1/4 teaspoon mixed spice

3/4 cup (90g) chopped pecans or walnuts

1/2 cup (25g) chopped flaked coconut

1/2 cup (85g) chopped raisins

1/2 cup (125g) chopped red glacé cherries

frosting

1 cup (220g) sugar

1/3 cup (80ml) water

2 egg whites

Grease two 20cm sandwich pans, line bases with baking paper; grease paper. Cream butter, essence and sugar with electric mixer until light and fluffy; beat in eggs one at a time. Stir in sifted flour and milk, in two batches. Spread mixture into prepared pans; bake in moderate oven for about 30 minutes. Turn cakes onto wire racks to cool.

Place one cake on serving plate, spread Filling evenly over cake, top with remaining cake. Cover and refrigerate for several hours. Spread with Frosting just before serving.

Filling Combine butter, sugar, brandy and the water in small saucepan; stir over heat until butter is melted and sugar is dissolved. Bring to a boil, then boil for 1 minute, uncovered, without stirring. Remove from heat, gradually whisk in egg until mixture thickens slightly. Transfer mixture to bowl, mix in remaining ingredients. Cover and refrigerate for several hours until mixture holds its shape.

Frosting Combine sugar and the water in small saucepan; stir over heat, without boiling, until sugar is dissolved. Bring to a boil, then boil rapidly, uncovered, without stirring, for about 3 to 5 minutes or until syrup reaches 115°C on a candy thermometer (the syrup should not change colour). Alternatively, drop 1 teaspoon syrup into cold water; it should form a ball of soft, sticky toffee when rolled between fingers. While syrup is boiling, beat egg whites in small bowl with electric mixer until soft peaks form. Add syrup to egg whites in thin stream, while beating on medium speed. Beat until frosting forms stiff peaks.

SERVES 10

Per serving 22.7g fat; 2189kJ

44 oven-steamed pudding

1 cup (150g)
dried currants

1 cup (160g) sultanas

1 cup (170g)
chopped raisins

1/2 cup (85g)
mixed peel

1/3 cup (55g) chopped
blanched almonds

185g butter

3/4 cup (150g) firmly
packed brown sugar

3 eggs

1 cup (70g) stale
breadcrumbs

3/4 cup (110g)
plain flour

1/2 teaspoon
bicarbonate of soda

1 teaspoon
ground cinnamon

1/2 teaspoon
ground nutmeg

1/3 cup (80ml) brandy

Grease 21cm baba pan, line with plastic wrap, trim edge.

Combine fruit and nuts in large bowl. Beat butter and sugar in small bowl with electric mixer until just combined. Add eggs, one at a time, beating until just combined between additions. Stir into fruit mixture, then stir in breadcrumbs, sifted dry ingredients and brandy.

Spread pudding mixture into prepared pan; cover pudding with greased foil. Place pan in baking dish with enough boiling water to come halfway up side of pan. Bake in moderate oven about 1 1/2 hours, adding more boiling water as necessary.

SERVES 10
Per serving 20.5g fat; 2034kJ

microwave puddings 45

We used a 600-watt microwave oven for this recipe.

2³/₄ cups (500g) mixed dried fruit

¹/₃ cup (80ml) brandy

125g butter

³/₄ cup (150g) firmly packed brown sugar

2 tablespoons golden syrup

2 eggs

1 teaspoon Parisian essence, optional

1 large (200g) apple, peeled, grated coarsely

³/₄ cup (110g) plain flour

2 teaspoons mixed spice

¹/₂ teaspoon bicarbonate of soda

Grease eight ³/₄-cup (180ml) microwave-safe dishes.
Combine fruit and brandy in another small microwave-safe bowl; cook, covered, on HIGH (100%) 1 minute.
Beat butter, sugar and syrup in small bowl with electric mixer until combined. Add eggs, one at a time, beating until just combined between additions, beat in essence. Transfer mixture to large bowl; stir in fruit mixture, apple and sifted dry ingredients.
Divide mixture evenly among prepared dishes, smooth tops.
Arrange dishes around edge of microwave turntable; cook, uncovered, on MEDIUM (50%) 10 minutes. Rotate dishes; cook on MEDIUM (50%) further 8 minutes or until centres of puddings are almost set. Stand puddings 10 minutes; centres of puddings should be firm. Turn puddings onto serving dishes.

MAKES 8
Per serving 15g fat; 1974kJ

46 triple nut pudding with
rum custard

You will need a 60cm square of unbleached calico for this recipe.
If cloth is new, soak it in cold water overnight. Next day, boil calico
for 20 minutes; rinse.

1½ cups (250g) raisins

1½ cups (250g) sultanas

¾ cup (110g) dried currants

¾ cup (125g) chopped
seeded dates

⅓ cup (85g) chopped red
glacé cherries

¼ cup (40g) chopped mixed peel

2 cups (250g) chopped pecans

¾ cup (120g) pine nuts

½ cup (85g) chopped Brazil nuts

1 tablespoon finely grated
lemon rind

½ cup (125ml) brandy

250g butter

2 cups (400g) firmly packed
brown sugar

5 eggs

4 cups (280g) stale breadcrumbs

1⅓ cups (200g) plain flour

½ cup (75g) plain flour, extra

rum custard

¼ cup (55g) sugar

4 egg yolks

1½ cups (375ml) milk

2 teaspoons cornflour

2 teaspoons water

¼ cup (60ml) thickened cream

½ teaspoon vanilla essence

1 tablespoon dark rum

Combine fruit, nuts, rind and brandy in large bowl, cover; stand overnight.
Beat butter and sugar in medium bowl with electric mixer until just
combined. Add eggs, one at a time, beating until just combined between
additions. Stir into fruit mixture, then stir in breadcrumbs and flour.
Dip prepared pudding cloth in boiling water; boil 1 minute. Wearing
rubber gloves, squeeze water from cloth. Spread hot cloth on bench,
rub extra flour into centre of cloth to cover a 40cm area. Line large
bowl with the cloth, allowing edges to hang over sides; place mixture
into centre. Gather cloth around pudding mixture. Tie cloth tightly with
kitchen string close to mixture. Tie a loop in string.
Lower pudding into boiling water, cover with tight lid; boil rapidly
6 hours. Replenish boiling water as needed.

Place handle of wooden spoon through loop in string, lift pudding from water. Suspend pudding to swing freely. Twist wet ends of cloth away from pudding; hang for about 10 minutes or until cloth is dry. Place pudding in large bowl, cut string; peel back cloth a little. Invert onto plate, slowly peel cloth back completely; cool. Serve pudding with Rum Custard.

Rum Custard Beat sugar and egg yolks in small bowl with electric mixer until thick and creamy. Bring milk to a boil in medium saucepan, whisk into egg yolk mixture. Return to pan with blended cornflour and water; stir over low heat until custard boils and thickens slightly. Remove pan from heat; stir in cream, essence and rum.

SERVES 12
MAKES 2 cups (500ml) rum custard
Per serving pudding: 47.6g fat; 4011kJ custard (per tbsp): 2.5g fat; 172kJ

48 frozen

chestnut pudding

1/2 cup (85g) raisins,
chopped coarsely

1/3 cup (70g) red
glacé cherries,
chopped coarsely

1/3 cup (85g) chopped
glacé apricots

2/3 cup (110g) chopped
seeded dates

1/4 cup (60ml) rum

3 eggs

1/3 cup (75g)
caster sugar

250g can chestnut
spread

600ml thickened
cream

Combine fruit and rum in small bowl, cover; stand overnight.
Oil 1.5-litre (6-cup) pudding steamer.
Whisk eggs and sugar in medium bowl over saucepan of simmering water
until slightly thickened and frothy. Remove from heat; stir in chestnut
spread, cool to room temperature. Stir chestnut mixture into fruit mixture.
Beat cream in small bowl with electric mixer until soft peaks form;
fold into fruit mixture.
Pour mixture into prepared steamer, cover; freeze overnight.

SERVES 8
Per serving 30.1g fat; 2079kJ

sago steamed pudding

1/2 cup (100g) sago

2 cups (500ml) milk

60g butter

1 teaspoon finely grated lemon rind

2 cups (400g) firmly packed brown sugar

2 eggs

2 cups (375g) mixed dried fruit

4 cups (280g) stale breadcrumbs

1/2 teaspoon bicarbonate of soda

2 teaspoons mixed spice

Combine sago and milk in small bowl; stand 1 hour.

Grease 2-litre (8-cup) pudding steamer, line base with baking paper.

Beat butter, rind, sugar and eggs in small bowl with electric mixer until combined. Transfer mixture to large bowl; stir in sago mixture, fruit, breadcrumbs, soda and spice.

Pour mixture into prepared steamer; cover pudding with greased foil, secure with lid or kitchen string. Place steamer in large saucepan with enough boiling water to come halfway up side of steamer; simmer, covered, about 4 hours, adding more boiling water as necessary.

SERVES 12
Per serving 7.9g fat; 1673kJ

50 allergy-free
pudding

This recipe is gluten-free, contains no dairy products or eggs, and makes one cake or pudding.

2¼ cups (360g) sultanas

1½ cups (250g) chopped raisins

½ cup (75g) dried currants

1½ cups (250g) chopped seeded dates

1½ cups (375ml) water

½ cup (125ml) orange juice

2 tablespoons honey

1 cup (200g) firmly packed brown sugar

185g dairy-free margarine

1 cup (125g) soy flour

1 cup (150g) rice flour

1 teaspoon cream of tartar

½ teaspoon bicarbonate of soda

2 teaspoons mixed spice

1 cup (125g) almond meal

Combine fruit, the water, juice, honey, sugar and margarine in large saucepan. Stir over heat, without boiling, until margarine melts. Transfer mixture to large heatproof bowl; cool.

Grease 2.25-litre (9-cup) pudding steamer, line base with baking paper.

Stir sifted dry ingredients and almond meal into fruit mixture.

Spoon mixture into prepared steamer, cover pudding with greased foil; secure with lid or kitchen string. Place steamer in large saucepan with enough boiling water to come halfway up side of steamer; simmer, covered, about 6 hours, adding more boiling water as necessary.

SERVES 10
Per serving 23g fat; 2770kJ

Cake

Grease deep 19cm-square cake pan, line base and sides with three layers baking paper, extending paper 5cm above edge of pan.

Complete cake mixture following instructions above, then spread mixture into prepared pan; bake in slow oven about 2$\frac{1}{2}$ hours, covering loosely with foil after 1 hour. Cover hot cake tightly with foil; cool in pan.

SERVES 10
Per serving 23g fat; 2770kJ

52 fruity
christmas bombe

2 litres vanilla
ice-cream, softened

⅓ cup (75g) chopped
glacé pineapple

⅓ cup (85g) chopped
glacé apricots

⅓ cup (70g) red glacé
cherries, halved

¼ cup (50g) chopped
glacé ginger

1 teaspoon
mixed spice

1 teaspoon ground
cinnamon

700g packet rich
fruit cake

brandy cream sauce

300ml thickened
cream

¼ cup (60ml) brandy

2 eggs, separated

½ cup (110g)
caster sugar

Oil 1.75-litre (7-cup) pudding steamer, line
with plastic wrap.
Combine ice-cream, fruit, ginger and spices
in large bowl. Spoon mixture into prepared
steamer, cover; freeze about 1 hour or until firm.
Split cake in half, cut halves to fit on top of ice-
cream in steamer, press on gently. Cover; freeze
overnight. Serve with Brandy Cream Sauce.
Brandy Cream Sauce Beat cream and brandy
in small bowl with electric mixer until soft peaks
form. Beat egg whites in separate small bowl
with electric mixer until soft peaks form,
gradually add sugar, beating well between
additions. Add egg yolks; beat well. Fold
cream mixture into egg white mixture.

SERVES 8
Per serving 23.4g fat; 2564kJ

economical steamed
pudding

2 pot-strength
tea bags

1 cup (250ml)
boiling water

2 cups (375g) mixed
dried fruit

1 cup (200g) firmly
packed brown sugar

1 egg, beaten lightly

2 cups (300g)
self-raising flour

1 teaspoon
ground cinnamon

1 teaspoon
ground nutmeg

Combine tea bags and the water in heatproof
jug; stand 5 minutes. Discard tea bags, cool
tea to room temperature. Combine fruit and tea
in large bowl, cover; stand overnight.

Grease 1.5-litre (6-cup) pudding steamer, line
base with baking paper.

Add remaining ingredients to fruit mixture.
Spoon mixture into prepared steamer; cover
pudding with baking paper, then foil, secure
with lid or kitchen string. Place steamer in large
saucepan with enough boiling water to come
halfway up side of steamer; simmer, covered,
about 3 hours, adding more boiling water as
necessary. Stand 5 minutes before turning out.

SERVES 8
Per serving 1.7g fat; 1490kJ

54 australian

christmas pudding

½ cup (125g) finely
chopped glacé apricots

½ cup (125g) finely
chopped glacé peaches

2 tablespoons (35g)
finely chopped red
glacé cherries

2 tablespoons (35g)
finely chopped green
glacé cherries

¼ cup (40g) sultanas

¼ cup (60ml) brandy

2 teaspoons gelatine

1 tablespoon water

4 eggs, separated

½ cup (80g) icing
sugar mixture

¼ cup (25g)
cocoa powder

60g dark chocolate,
melted

⅓ cup (50g) hazelnuts,
chopped coarsely

50g chocolate-coated
honeycomb bar,
chopped coarsely

300ml thickened cream

100g white chocolate
Melts, melted

Combine fruit and brandy in large bowl,
cover; stand overnight.

Grease 1.375-litre (5½-cup) pudding
steamer, line with plastic wrap.

Sprinkle gelatine over the water in cup,
stand in small pan of simmering water, stir
until dissolved; cool.

Beat egg whites in medium bowl with
electric mixer until firm peaks form,
gradually beat in sifted combined icing
sugar and cocoa. Fold in lightly beaten
egg yolks and cooled dark chocolate.

Stir gelatine mixture, nuts and chocolate
honeycomb into fruit mixture; fold in
chocolate mixture. Beat cream in small bowl
with electric mixer until soft peaks form,
fold into fruit mixture. Pour mixture into
prepared steamer. Cover; freeze overnight.

Just before serving, turn pudding onto
serving plate; smooth surface with wet
hands. Spoon white chocolate over the top.

SERVES 12
Per serving 19g fat; 1463kJ

56 light steamed pudding

185g butter

1 tablespoon finely grated orange rind

1 cup (200g) firmly packed brown sugar

3 eggs

1½ cups (250g) sultanas

½ cup (105g) glacé cherries, halved

¾ cup (125g) chopped dried mango

¾ cup (110g) chopped dried apricots

⅓ cup (80ml) orange juice

1 cup (150g) plain flour

½ cup (75g) self-raising flour

2 teaspoons mixed spice

2 cups (140g) stale breadcrumbs

Grease 2.25-litre (9-cup) pudding steamer, line base with baking paper.

Beat butter, rind and sugar in small bowl with electric mixer until just combined. Add eggs, one at a time, beating until just combined between additions. Transfer mixture to large bowl, add fruit and juice, mix well. Stir in flours and spice, then breadcrumbs.

Spoon mixture into prepared steamer; cover pudding with greased foil, secure with lid or kitchen string. Place steamer in large saucepan with enough boiling water to come halfway up side of steamer; simmer, covered, about 3 hours, adding more boiling water as necessary. Stand 20 minutes before turning out.

SERVES 10
Per serving 17.9g fat; 2196kJ

christmas puddings

2 cups (375g) mixed
dried fruit

1/4 cup (60g) chopped
glacé peaches

1/4 cup (60g) chopped
glacé apricots

1/4 cup (60ml) brandy

3/4 cup (110g)
macadamias, toasted,
chopped finely

1 teaspoon
mixed spice

1 teaspoon ground
cinnamon

2 litres good quality
vanilla ice-cream,
softened

1 cup (150g) white
chocolate Melts,
melted

Combine fruit and brandy in large bowl; cover,
stand overnight.

Line bases of eight 1-cup (250ml) freezer-proof
moulds (we used tea cups) with baking paper.

Stir nuts, spices and ice-cream into fruit
mixture. Divide mixture among prepared
moulds, cover; freeze overnight.

Turn puddings onto tray, peel away baking
paper. Spoon melted white Melts into a small
plastic bag, then snip off the corner of the bag.
Drizzle the melted chocolate over the puddings.

SERVES 8
Per serving 30.5g fat; 2543kJ

58 pineapple rum
christmas pudding

450g can crushed pineapple in heavy syrup

250g butter, chopped coarsely

1 cup (200g) firmly packed brown sugar

1½ cups (250g) sultanas

1½ cups (250g) chopped raisins

¾ cup (125g) chopped seeded dates

¾ cup (110g) dried currants

⅓ cup (85g) chopped red glacé cherries

4 eggs, beaten lightly

¾ cup (110g) plain flour

¾ cup (110g) self-raising flour

½ cup (35g) stale breadcrumbs

rum syrup

½ cup (110g) sugar

½ cup (125ml) rum

butterscotch sauce

½ cup (100g) firmly packed brown sugar

125g butter, chopped coarsely

1 cup (250ml) cream

½ cup (125ml) reserved Rum Syrup

Drain pineapple well, reserve ½ cup (125ml) of pineapple syrup. Place pineapple on absorbent paper, pat dry. Combine butter and sugar in large saucepan. Stir over heat, without boiling, until sugar dissolves. Stir in half of the Rum Syrup, bring to a boil; remove from heat. Stir in all fruit and pineapple. Transfer mixture to large bowl; cool. Grease 2.25-litre (9-cup) pudding steamer, line base with baking paper. Stir egg, flours and breadcrumbs into fruit mixture. Spoon mixture into prepared steamer; cover pudding with greased foil, secure with lid or kitchen string. Place steamer in large saucepan with enough boiling water to come halfway up side of steamer; simmer, covered, about 6 hours, adding more boiling water as necessary. Stand 20 minutes before turning out; serve with Butterscotch Sauce.

Rum Syrup Heat sugar in medium frying pan, stirring, until dissolved and browned. Add rum and reserved pineapple syrup (mixture will bubble); cook, stirring, until toffee is dissolved.

Butterscotch Sauce Combine ingredients in medium saucepan, stir over heat, until sugar is dissolved and butter melts.

SERVES 12
MAKES 2½ cups (625ml) butterscotch sauce
Per serving pudding: 19.5g fat; 2375kJ
butterscotch sauce (per tbsp): 7.1g fat; 367kJ

glossary

allspice also known as pimento or Jamaican pepper; available whole or ground. Tastes like a blend of cinnamon, clove and nutmeg.

almond meal also known as ground almonds.

baking powder a raising agent consisting mainly of two parts cream of tartar to one part bicarbonate of soda (baking soda).

bicarbonate of soda also known as baking soda.

breadcrumbs

stale: one- or two-day-old bread made into crumbs by grating, blending or processing.

cheese

cream: soft milk cheese commonly known as "Philadelphia" or "Philly".

chestnut spread also known as Sweetened Chestnut Puree or Creme de Marrons; a French product made of pureed chestnuts, candied chestnut pieces, sugar, glucose syrup and vanilla. Available from good delicatessens; not to be confused with Chestnut Puree, made only of pureed chestnuts and water.

chocolate

-coated honeycomb bar: we used a Violet Crumble bar.

dark: eating chocolate; made of cocoa liquor, cocoa butter and sugar.

Choc Bits: also known as chocolate chips and chocolate morsels; available in milk, white and dark chocolate. Made of cocoa liquor, cocoa butter, sugar and an emulsifier, these hold their shape in baking and are ideal for decorating.

white Melts: discs of compounded white chocolate ideal for melting or moulding.

Cointreau citrus-flavoured liqueur.

cornflour also known as cornstarch.

cream

fresh: also known as pure cream and pouring cream, and has a minimum fat content of 35%; has no additives like commercially thickened cream.

sour: a thick, commercially cultured, soured cream (minimum fat content 35%); good for dips, toppings and baked cheesecakes.

thickened: a whipping cream (minimum fat content 35%) containing a thickener.

cream of tartar ingredient in baking powder; sometimes added to confectionery mixtures to help prevent sugar from crystallising.

custard

powder: packaged, vanilla pudding mixture.

prepared: (vanilla) pouring custard, available in cartons.

essence extract.

flour

rice: flour ground from rice grains.

soy: creamy flour processed from soy beans.

white plain: an all-purpose flour, made from wheat.

white self-raising: plain flour sifted with baking powder in the proportion of 1 cup flour to 2 teaspoons baking powder.

wholemeal plain: wholewheat flour.

wholemeal self-raising: wholewheat flour with the addition of baking powder.

food colourings available in liquid, powdered and concentrated paste forms.

gelatine (gelatin) we used powdered gelatine. It is also available in sheet form known as leaf gelatine.

golden syrup a by-product of refined sugar cane; pure maple syrup or honey can be substituted.

Grand Marnier orange-flavoured liqueur based on Cognac-brandy.

hazelnut meal ground hazelnuts.

Irish cream we used Baileys Original Irish Cream, based on Irish whiskey, spirits and cream.

jam also known as preserve or conserve; most often made from fruit.

macadamias rich, buttery nuts; store in refrigerator due to high fat content.

maple syrup distilled sap of the maple tree; maple-flavoured syrup is no substitute for maple syrup.

marsala a sweet fortified wine originally from Sicily.

marzipan made from sugar, almonds and glucose.

milk we used full-cream homogenised milk unless otherwise specified.

sweetened condensed: a canned milk product consisting of milk with more than half the water content removed and sugar added to the milk which remains.

mixed peel candied citrus peel.

mixed spice a blend of ground spices usually consisting of cinnamon, allspice and nutmeg.

Nutella chocolate hazelnut spread.

parisian essence used to give a rich brown colour in cakes, puddings and soups.

pumpkin also known as squash, the pumpkin is a member of the gourd family used in cooking both as one of many ingredients in a dish or eaten on its own. Various types can be substituted for one another.

soft icing packaged ready-to-roll fondant, available from some supermarkets and specialty cake decorating shops.

sago also known as seed or pearl tapioca, it is from the sago palm. Used in soups and desserts, often as a thickening agent.

sugar we used coarse, granulated table sugar, also known as crystal sugar, unless otherwise specified.

brown: an extremely soft, fine granulated sugar retaining molasses for its characteristic colour and flavour.

caster: also known as superfine or finely granulated table sugar.

demerara: small-grained golden-coloured crystal sugar.

pure icing: also known as confectioners' sugar or powdered sugar.

icing sugar mixture: also known as confectioners' sugar or powdered sugar; granulated sugar crushed together with a small amount (about 3%) cornflour added.

raw: natural brown granulated sugar.

sultanas golden raisins.

treacle thick, dark syrup not unlike molasses; a by-product from sugar refining.

62 index

facts and figures 63

These conversions are approximate only, but the difference between an exact and the approximate conversion of various liquid and dry measures is minimal and will not affect your cooking results.

Measuring equipment
The difference between one country's measuring cups and another's is, at most, within a 2 or 3 teaspoon variance. (For the record, 1 Australian metric measuring cup holds approximately 250ml.) The most accurate way of measuring dry ingredients is to weigh them. For liquids, use a clear glass or plastic jug having metric markings.

Note: NZ, Canada, USA and UK all use 15ml tablespoons. Australian tablespoons measure 20ml.
All cup and spoon measurements are level.

How to measure
When using graduated measuring cups, shake dry ingredients loosely into the appropriate cup. Do not tap the cup on a bench or tightly pack the ingredients unless directed to do so. Level the top of measuring cups and measuring spoons with a knife. When measuring liquids, place a clear glass or plastic jug having metric markings on a flat surface to check accuracy at eye level.

Dry Measures

metric	imperial
15g	1/2oz
30g	1oz
60g	2oz
90g	3oz
125g	4oz (1/4lb)
155g	5oz
185g	6oz
220g	7oz
250g	8oz (1/2lb)
280g	9oz
315g	10oz
345g	11oz
375g	12oz (3/4lb)
410g	13oz
440g	14oz
470g	15oz
500g	16oz (1lb)
750g	24oz (1 1/2lb)
1kg	32oz (2lb)

We use large eggs having an average weight of 60g.

Liquid Measures

metric	imperial
30ml	1 fluid oz
60ml	2 fluid oz
100ml	3 fluid oz
125ml	4 fluid oz
150ml	5 fluid oz (1/4 pint/1 gill)
190ml	6 fluid oz
250ml (1cup)	8 fluid oz
300ml	10 fluid oz (1/2 pint)
500ml	16 fluid oz
600ml	20 fluid oz (1 pint)
1000ml (1litre)	1 3/4 pints

Helpful Measures

metric	imperial
3mm	1/8in
6mm	1/4in
1cm	1/2in
2cm	3/4in
2.5cm	1in
6cm	2 1/2in
8cm	3in
20cm	8in
23cm	9in
25cm	10in
30cm	12in (1ft)

Oven Temperatures
These oven temperatures are only a guide. Always check the manufacturer's manual.

	°C (Celsius)	°F (Fahrenheit)	Gas Mark
Very slow	120	250	1
Slow	150	300	2
Moderately slow	160	325	3
Moderate	180 – 190	350 – 375	4
Moderately hot	200 – 210	400 – 425	5
Hot	220 – 230	450 – 475	6
Very hot	240 – 250	500 – 525	7

at your fingertips

These elegant slipcovers store up to 10 mini books and make the books instantly accessible.

And the metric measuring cups and spoons make following our recipes a piece of cake.

Book Holder
Australia and overseas:
$A8.95 (incl. GST).

Metric Measuring Set
Australia: $6.50 (incl. GST).
New Zealand: $A8.00.
Elsewhere: $A9.95.
Prices include postage
and handling.
This offer is available
in all countries.

Photocopy and complete the coupon below

Mail or fax Photocopy and complete the coupon below and post to ACP Books Reader Offer, ACP Publishing, GPO Box 4967, Sydney NSW 2001, *or* fax to (02) 9267 4967.

Phone Have your credit card details ready, then phone 136 116 (Mon-Fri, 8.00am – 6.00pm; Sat 8.00am – 6.00pm).

Australian residents We accept the credit cards listed on the coupon, money orders and cheques.

Overseas residents We accept the credit cards listed on the coupon, drafts in $A drawn on an Australian bank, and also British, New Zealand and U.S. cheques in the currency of the country of issue. Credit card charges are at the exchange rate current at the time of payment.

☐ **Book holder**   ☐ **Metric measuring set**
Please indicate number(s) required.

Mr/Mrs/Ms _____

Address _____

_____

Postcode _____ Country_____

Phone: Business hours (   ) _____

I enclose my cheque/money order for $_____ payable to ACP Publishing

OR: please charge $ _____ to my: ☐ Bankcard   ☐ Visa
☐ American Express   ☐ MasterCard   ☐ Diners Club

Expiry Date ___/___

☐☐☐☐☐☐☐☐☐☐☐☐☐☐☐☐☐☐

Cardholder's signature _____

Please allow up to 30 days for delivery within Australia.
Allow up to 6 weeks for overseas deliveries. Both offers expire 31/12/03.
HLMCCAP02

Food director Pamela Clark
Associate food editor Karen Hammial
Assistant food editor Kathy McGarry
Assistant recipe editor Elizabeth Hooper

ACP BOOKS STAFF
Editorial director Susan Tomnay
Editor Julie Collard
Concept design Jackie Richards
Designer Mary Keep
Publishing manager (sales) Jennifer McDona
**Publishing manager
(rights & new titles)** Jane Hazell
Production manager Carol Currie

Publisher Sue Wannan
Group publisher Jill Baker
Chief executive officer John Alexander

Produced by ACP Books, Sydney.

Colour separations by
ACP Colour Graphics Pty Ltd, Sydney.
Printing by Dai Nippon Printing in Hong Kong

Published by ACP Publishing Pty Limited,
54 Park St, Sydney; GPO Box 4088, Sydney,
NSW 1028. Ph: (02) 9282 8618
Fax: (02) 9267 9438.

To order books, phone 136 116.
acpbooks@acp.com.au
www.acpbooks.com.au

Australia Distributed by Network Services,
GPO Box 4088, Sydney, NSW 1028.
Ph: (02) 9282 8777 Fax: (02) 9264 3278.

United Kingdom Distributed by Australian
Consolidated Press (UK), Moulton Park Busine
Centre, Red House Road, Moulton Park,
Northampton, NN3 6AQ. Ph: (01604) 497 531.
Fax: (01604) 497 533 acpukltd@aol.com

Canada Distributed by Whitecap Books Ltd,
351 Lynn Ave, North Vancouver, BC, V7J 2C4.
Ph: (604) 980 9852.

New Zealand Distributed by Netlink Distributior
Company, Level 4, 23 Hargreaves St,
College Hill, Auckland 1. Ph: (9) 302 7616.

Clark, Pamela.
Christmas Cakes & Puddings.

Includes index.
ISBN 1 86396 204 2

1. Christmas Cookery. 2. Christmas Cakes.
3. Plum Puddings.
I. Title: Australian Women's Weekly.
(Series: Australian Women's Weekly
Sweet and Simple mini series).

641.568

© ACP Publishing Pty Limited 2000
ABN 18 053 273 546

First published 2000. Reprinted 2002.

Cover: Australian Christmas pudding, page 54.
Stylist: Sarah O'Brien
Photographer: Scott Cameron
Back cover: Little frozen Christmas
puddings, page 57.

The publishers would like to thank Accoutremen
Acorn Trading, Country Road Homewares and
The Bay Tree Kitchen Shop for props used in
photography.